Corona Poems

Corona Poems

DAVID JAFFIN

First published in the United Kingdom in 2020 by
Shearsman Books
50 Westons Hill Drive
Emersons Green
Bristol BS16 7DF

Shearsman Books Ltd Registered Office
30–31 St. James Place, Mangotsfield, Bristol BS16 9JB
(this address not for correspondence)

www.shearsman.com

ISBN 978-1-84861-682-0

Distributed for Shearsman Books in the U. S. A.
by Small Press Distribution, 1341 Seventh Avenue, Berkeley, CA 94710
E-Mail orders@spdbooks.org
www.spdbooks.org

Production, composition, & cover design: Edition Wortschatz,
a service of Neufeld Verlag, Cuxhaven/Germany
E-Mail info@edition-wortschatz.de, www.edition-wortschatz.de

Title illustration:
"Geheimnisvolles Wachstum/Mysterious Growth",
by Hannelore Bäumler, München

Printed in Germany

Contents

With continuing thanks for
Marina Moisel
preparing
this manuscript

and to Hanni Bäumler
for her well-placed
photograph

If I had to classify my poetry, it could best be done through the classical known "saying the most by using the least". The aim is thereby set: transparency, clarity, word-purity. Every word must carry its weight in the line and the ultimate aim is a unity of sound, sense, image and idea. Poetry, more than any other art, should seek for a unity of the senses, as the French Symbolists, the first poetic modernists, realized through the interchangeability of the senses: "I could hear the colors of her dress." One doesn't hear colors, but nevertheless there is a sensual truth in such an expression.

Essential is "saying the most by using the least". Compression is of the essence. And here are some of my most personal means of doing so turning verbs into nouns and the reverse, even within a double-context "Why do the leaves her so ungenerously behind". Breaking words into two or even three parts to enable both compression and the continuing flow of meaning. Those words must be placed back together again, thereby revealing their inner structure-atomising.

One of my critics rightly said: "Jaffin's poetry is everywhere from one seemingly unrelated poem to the next." Why? Firstly because of my education and interests trained at New York University as a cultural and intellectual historian. My doctoral dissertation on historiography emphasizes the necessary historical continuity. Today we often judge the past with the mind and mood of the present, totally contrary to their own historical context. I don't deny the past-romanticism and classical but integrate them within a singular modern context of word-usage and sensibility. Musically that would place me within the "classical-romantic tradition" of Haydn, Mozart, Mendelssohn, Brahms and Nielsen but at the very modern end of that tradition.

My life historically is certainly exceptional. My father was a prominent New York Jewish lawyer. The law never interested me, but history always did. A career as a cultural-intellectual historian was mine-for-the-asking, but I rejected historical relativism. That led me to a marriage with a devout German lady – so I took to a calling of Jesus-the-Jew in post-Auschwitz Germany. For ca. two decades I wrote and lectured all over Germany on Jesus the Jew. Thereby my knowledge and understanding of both interlocked religions became an essential part of my being. History, faith and religion two sides of me but also art, classical music and literature were of essential meaning – so many poems on poetry, classical music and painting.

Then Rosemarie and I have been very happily married for 59 years now. Impossible that a German and Jew could be so happily married so shortly after the war? I've written love poems for her, hundreds and hundreds over those 59 years, not only the love poems, as most are, of the first and often unfulfilling passion, but "love and marriage go together like a horse and carriage". Perhaps too prosaic for many poets?

When did I become a poet? My sister Lois wrote reasonably good poetry as an adolescent. I, only interested in sports until my Bar Mitzvah, a tournament tennis and table-tennis player, coached baseball and basketball teams, also soccer.

My sister asked whether I'd ever read Dostoyevsky.
I'd only read John R. Tunis sports books and the
sports section of the *New York Times* so I answered
"in which sports was he active?" She said, rather con-
descendingly, "If you haven't read Dostoyevsky, you
haven't lived." So I went to the library for the very
first time and asked for a book by this Dostoyevsky.
I received *Poor People*, his first book, that made him
world famous. My mother shocked to see me read-
ing and most especially a book about poor people
said, "David, don't read that it will make you sad,
unhappy – we, living in Scarsdale, weren't after all,
poor people. From there it went quickly to my Tol-
stoy, Hardy and so on. In music it started with the hit
parade, then *Lost in the Stars*, then the popular classics
and with 15 or 16 my Haydn, Mozart, Schütz, Vic-
toria… And then at Ann Arbor and NYU to my art-
ists, most especially Giovanni Bellini, Van der Wey-
den, Georges de la Tour, Corot and Gauguin…

But it was Wallace Stevens' reading in the early 50s
in the YMHA that set me off – he didn't read very
well, but his 13 Ways of Looking at a Blackbird, Idea
of Order at Key West, Two Letters (in *Poems Posthu-
mous*), Peter Quince at the Clavier, The Snowman…
and the excellent obituary in *Time* magazine plus the
letter he answered some of my poems with compli-
ments but "you must be your own hardest critic".
That pre-determined my extremely self-critical way
with a poem. Please don't believe that prolific means
sloppy, for I'm extremely meticulous with each and
every poem.

My poems were published in the order written and I'm way ahead of any counting… The poem is a dia-logical process as everything in life. The words come to me not from me, and if they strike or possibly join-a-union then I become desparate, read long-winded poets like Paz to set me off – he's very good at odd times. Those poems need my critical mood-mind as much as I need their very specially chosen words – not the "magic words" of the romantics, but the cleansed words of Jaffin – Racine used only 500 words. My words too are a specially limited society, often used, but in newly-felt contexts.

O something very special: I have a terrible poetic memory. If I had a good one as presumably most poets, I'd write say one poem about a butterfly, and every time I see/saw a butterfly it would be that one, that poem. But I forget my poems, so each butter-fly, lizard, squirrel… is other-placed, other-mooded, other-worded, other-Jaffined. That's the main reason why I am most certainly the most prolific of all poets.

Shakespeare is the greatest of us: his sonnets live most from the fluency and density of his language. I advise all future poets to keep away from his influence and the poetic greatness of The Bible.

Yours truly
David Jaffin

P. S.: As a preacher the truth (Christ) should become straight-lined, timelessly so, but as a poet it's quite different. What interests me most are those contradictions which live deeply within all of us, not only in theory, but daily in the practice. And then the romantics have led me to those off-sided thoroughly poetic truths that mysteriously not knowing where that darkened path will lead us.

Poetry Book 98

If room

> s can't speak
> why does each
>
> possess a voice-
> of-its-own
>
> so distinct
> that one's
>
> own receptiv
> ity alter
>
> s from each
> to each.

What need

> of art museum
> s when each
>
> still winter
> ing tree on
>
> the way e
> vokes an in
>
> dividual pre-
> conceived
>
> expressive
> ness.

Spring tulip

> s bunched to
> such varied
>
> coloring
> s that may
>
> have been
> contrapunct
>
> ually birth
> ed.

When picture (4)

> *a) s by the same*
>
> artist start
>
> and continue
> looking much–
>
>
> *b) the-same it*
>
> could be by
>
> displaying
> an authent
>
> ic genuine
> sense of pur

c) posing or

that they'

ve derived
from a pre-

given scheme
or because

d) the painter'

s lacking a

diversity
of poetic-ex

pressive
ness.

Heavenly (4)

a) Imitation

s This immov

able assem
blage of cloud

b) s seems to be

preparing for

a conference
of consider

able import

c) ance while we'

ve only exper
ienced an al

most devout re
verence as if

d) the heavens

were proclaim

ing a distant
but still divine

ly-felt revela
tion.

As the Corona (3)

a) virus remain

s particular

ly dangerous
for the old

and weakened

b) does its mess

age imply the
survival of

the fittest
or are its

victims just

c) most natural

ly selected
because their

lengthened
time's now fin

ally-up.

5:15 only (2)

a) the moon so

intensely–mag

netically–
bright I could

n't look away
It took–hold

b) of my very–

being witness

ing more–of–
me than I'd

ever self–i
magined.

Early March (3)

a) off-season at

Illmensee

our small e
lusively con

b) templative

lake now en

compassing
its darkness

depthed for
the summer'

c) s surfacing

upon that re–
establish
ing express

iveness.

Remembrances (4)

a) He said "I

want to be re
membered in

other ways

b) than just as

a poetical a
side" My father

preferred his
engraved name

c) on his univer

sity and hospi

tal plague
s But "what'

s in a name"
buried among

d) those others

now anonymous

ly grave–stone
d forgetful

ness.

Fading-outs

That once so
brightly appar

ent moon's
now eased down

to the hori
zoned cloud–

encompassing
invisibly

timely fad
ing-out

s.

Only now (2)

a) do I realize

that the tree'

s ever-green
or timely

leafed–bare
nesses the

b) through-writt

en self-deci

phering alpha
bet of The

Good Lord's
most creative-

urgings.

The lake *(2)*

a) kept drifting

my thought

s beyond
reach of their

word-impend
ing poetical

b) ly-certained

self-sustain

ing here and
nowheres-else.

Why are these (2)

    a) hand-made self-

sufficient

bird house
s so tiny

holed that it
becomes hard

    b) to imagine

even the small

est of domest
ic-further

ings comfort
ably fitting–

through.

Why at the (3)

    a) Lake of Constance

's promenade

s filled with
sun-hungry

appreciative

b) early spring

attendant–
families where

as on the lake
itself only a

vast void

c) Not a single

pleasure boat
timed for such

seasonably ap
parent surfa

cings.

Answering– (3)

a) back It's be

come hard to

distinguish
these early

b) March transit

ional time

s between late
winter and early

spring though
those multi-

c) colored grass

ed stream-lin

ed flowers
suddenly una

wares answer
ing-back.

Some women (2)

a) may feel some

thing of an

otherwise-
self in new

ly acquired

b) clothes espec

ially those
which cover

the full–length
of their self–

imagining
s.

In the sub (2)

a) way the 3-of-us

(2 very little
boys with bright

blue balloon
s and myself)

b) played hide and

seek though I

never found
anything else

than those
soul–blue ap

pearance
s.

Love-grooming (5)

a) Many of the

middle-age wo
men here are

either fat
enough to ap

b) pear at odd

times almost

jovial Other
s with that

staid used–

c) out-look where

as my almost
82-year-old

Rosemarie

d) remains as if

she's about
to celebrate

her 27th birth

e) day because

(as I usually
maintain) of

my daily love–
grooming.

All of these (3)

a) mostly ground-

based pretti

fying flower
s colored in

b) various fla

vours can't

convince me
with these

daily pene
trating cold

c) winds that

spring's act

ually (if only
half-permanent

ly) arrived.

Thanks to the (4)

a) "Chinese" Corona

virus major

soccer game
s will be

b) played-out

only for emp

ty seats and
even the opera

with its pedi

c) gree appeal

will become
staged for

a non–appar
ent audience

c) (which may be

come invisibly–

present if
only ghostly–

sanctioned).

Thematic (3)

a) poems may be

come more-than-

enhanced with
an inclusive

b) title but if

failing to ap

pear like a
business man

who has missed
his train but

c) made sure be

fore leaving

not to forget
his top-seat

ed hat again.

Some need (6)

 a) more-of-this

 others more-

 of-that It
 must be hard

 b) for many wo

 men to accept

 Lady Chatterly'
 s lover as an

 ideal–mate

 c) but equally

 difficult
 to be fully

 satisfied
 with her plat

d) onic husband

Some need more–

of-this other
s more-of-

that but even
while possess

e) ing both may

not realize

a truly success
ful-relation

ship There

f) still remain

s something
more than

this or even
that.

When he got (2)

> *a) wound-up with*

his 5–stoned

sling-shot
as David the

poet-king
he could not

> *b) only hit*

Goliath at his

death-bringing
place but also

untold other
wise-victim

s.

These wind (3)

> *a) blown cloud*
>
> s have been
>
> moving through
> my conscious
>
>
> *b) ness I can't*
>
> realize their
>
> speed–drift
> or direction
>
> but I do know
> it's going to
>
>
> *c) be a self-*
>
> satisfying
>
> ride if only
> for a shorten
>
> ed length-
> span.

Little girl *(5)*

a) s skipping a

round Miss Ol

son's 3rd grade
music room'

s circular

b) activating

imitation
of a life–

growth freed
om-find cyl

cle Where does

c) this endless

space actual
ly end or is

it simply cir
cling around

itself without

d) start or fin

ish as an A
siatic view

of time It's
perhaps more

appropriate

e) to ask why

many of us
seem to ex

perience

f) life in a

most similar
kind of self–

enclosing
way.

Poetic re (2)

a) mains for ex

ample why this

tree-branch–
house reflect

s such a mu

b) ted response

failing to
focus for more

than a life–
growth appar

ency.

The outside- (2)

   a) in and inside-

   out of a win

   dow's reflect
   ing view may

   deceive those

   b) ever-expect

   ant of a self–
   accomodating

   unity of
   dialogical–

   response.

Re-reading

      my Selected Poem
      s I must face–

      up to their ab
      stract simpli

      city of word-
      sense Has my

      form–control
      become too ef

      fusive.

It's not (6)

    a) possible even

in such a

short time-
span to dot

    b) all the i's

and cross the

numerous t'
s So much re

mains unanswer
ed and even

    c) sanctified

for the unspo

ken what could
have been

The Rankean
"as it actual

d) ly was" remain

s incomplete

all those un
dotted i's

and unreclaim
ing t's "Write-

e) it-out that

it won't be

forgotten The
medieval chron

ist uneased
until that win

f) tered-bare

tree becomes

fully colored
with its stead

ily increasing
birth–find.

He was what (4)

a) one refers to

as "a dedicat

ed scientist"
recognizing

b) his unusual

gifts at an

early age
always on the

scent for pro

c) blems and their

correspond
ing dialogi

cal answer
s even now in

his mid–80s

d) uneased by

his own self-
demanding

time-attend
ing gift

s.

For Tom (4)

a) Some very

selected per
sons have re

ceived the
gift of the

b) receptive

poetic-word

He an army
man and scien

tist untouch

c) ed by that poet

ic-word until
his 2nd wife'

s example and his
poetizing

friend helped

d) in his aging

years to an
inner growth

of unsuspect
ed self-find

ings.

This perhaps *(4)*

a) s less suscept

ible minor

tree nakedly
wintered only

b) at odd time

s partially

colored by
these tiny

wintering

c) birds sudden

ly unexpected
ly became pri

vileged with

d) totally self-en

compassing
brightly yellow

ed perform
ing–design

s.

Does there (7)

a) *still remain*

an invisible

line in some
late romantic

b) *music as Rachman*

inoff's 2nd

Piano Concerto
between what'

s deeply felt

c) *and still high-*

quality music
and what's act

ually more than
anything else

d) pulling-the-

heart's-string

ed-trash Is
that line an

e) objective

one or does

it remain
deeply subject

ive Why does it
remain necess

f) ary for me to

armour myself

against the
feelinged

claims of such

g) music Have I

remained at
heart's-length

a self-estab
lishing snob.

Perhaps we (4)

a) should question

why high-level

critics have
usually manag

b) ed to package

their own taste

as historical
ly-relevant

even canonic

c) whereas even

the greatest
of artist

s have often
felt doubt

d) s as to the

quality of

what they've
actually

achieved.

Corona (5)

a) Is our civili

sation so frag
ically sourced

that an invis
ible virus can

b) upset its very-

being political

ly socially e
conomically

personally

c) Is our so ad

vanced society
as helpless as

the 1348–49
generation

d) s plagued to

its very ground-

base And that
at a time when

e) we've so-to-

say become god

less master
s over life

and death.

Reestablish *(3)*

a) ing Love must

reestablish

itself through
often time-

b) holding look

s a most per

sonal touched-
expressive

ness and word

c) s that seem

to reach where
there's a comm

on receptive
blending–to

getherness.

Bon vivant *(12)*

a) It seemed as

if his had be
come a 4 or e

ven 5-timed
funeral mourned

by his past–
time lovers

b) each of when

seemed capable

of joining him
in that ever–

lasting death–
availing pit

c) "I'm the last

one" he confided
in me his min

ister after the
funeral He

d) meant the last

living one of

his class in
Malmsheim

I felt a kind
of companion

e) ship with him

being "the last

one" a Jew in
post-Auschwitz

Germany She

f) died quite

young but
fully endors

ed by her
mourning hus

band "You

g) should have ex

perienced how
receptive she

became after
only two drink

h) s" I didn't in

clude this exis

tencial most per
sonal endorse

ment in my fun
eral sermon.

i) Lasting-tradit

ions are often
strangely–sour

ed as in a
town in North

j) ern Württemberg

when the minister

in slippery late
November need

ed to jump over
that open grave

k) during the

final blessing

for fear of
falling in

himself Ever
since then

l) *that "blessing*

jump" has be

come a inte
gral part of

each and every
funeral.

Some of my (5)

a) *best character*

studies are of

those I best–
know Li Shang yin
b) remained bett

er equipped

to conceal
what and whom

he meant so as
not to get–on–

c) *the-wrong-side*

of friends and

supporter
s whereas my

personal
personae if

d) published at

all somewhere
half–lost in

the midst of

e) dozens of o

ther less ex
plicitly–

sourced poet
ic–insight

s.

Getting-out *(5)*

a) of-tough-situat

ion's easier

for those quick
and fluently

b) tongued but

getting into

such situation
s Usually pre

determined

c) by much the

same tempera
mentally spon

taneous person
But why did

d) I purchase for

our Spanish

teacher Lopez
early Arabic and

e) Jewish Andalu

sian poetry

but only in
German translat

ions.

Representat (4)

a) ional display

s If window

sills are often
used for repre

b) sentational

displays of

floral and o
ther seeting

s Why have

c) they usually

become room-o
riented and not

color-voiced

d) for the freed

om of the sky
s otherwise

changeable-
display

s.

The Corona *(4)*

a) virus has com

pletely shut-

down Italy
The shops

b) theatres con

certs and what

ever's afraid to
show their dis

illusioned
faces The street

c) s are mainly

vacant but strange

ly enough those
historical build

ings ancient med
ieval and other

d) wise have come

to life once

again haunting
that disease–

stricken coun
try.

This March

sun may be
bright but

it's a cold
brightness

as when that
stream's bar

ed-down to
its stone-re

flective ur
ging

s.

Word-sense (6)

a) Just as we

possess a
feel-sense

relative
to persons

b) places and

things in a

more cultivat
ed society

many realize
a word-sense

c) as an express

ive means of

certifying
what we've

acutally ex

d) perienced

Especially
women may

dress in such
a way to indi

e) cate something

of their self–

personed be
ing Few men

as Henry James
become equipp

f) ed with such

a personal

ly identify
ing word–

sense.

That night (2)

a) became window

ed in star

s sensed e
ven beyond

his limited
reach for a

b) self-perpetua

ting if dis

tantly spaced
immensely reali

zing aware
ness.

This ever-wit

nessing moon re
minds me more

of Odilon Redon'
s lonely boat

in the midst
of an uncer

tained al
most time

lessly appar
ent vacan

cy.

This may well

become the
third time

that Ingo'
s activating

faith has
closed that

heavily span
ed door upon

death's self-re
assuring claim

s.

During this *(4)*

a) Corona crisis

he became al

most daily a
ware of that

b) deadly plague-

written 1348–

49 year and
most especial

ly of that

c) death-overcom

ing ship with
its entire

crew Shakespear
ian–like flat

dead–down on

d) the deck and

only the sur
viving rat

s at its helm'
s-sake.

Why did the (7)

a) great colorist

Odilon Redon

begin his work
only in black

b) and white as

an unsuspect

ing prelude to
what's coming

next as Beethoven'

c) s string trios

preparing the
way for his

"important"
string quartet

s or wasn't Re

d) don himself fully

aware of his

especially
coloring-gift

s or didn't

e) he feel him

self fully-pre
pared for his

life-long feast-
of-color

e) s Were Redon'

s flowers so

singular in
their finely

sensed–express

f) iveness because

they weren't
"real" flower

s but only the

g) impression

of what could–
have–been seld

om–flower
ings.

Trumpism *(2)*

a) The real

gift of succ

ess in what
ever field

is to induce
or even force

b) others to

play within the
rules of your

game and not
their self–

sponsored
ones.

"Bewitched *(2)*

a) bothered and

bewildered"

from a once
popular song

describing

b) the actual

symptoms of
that alway

s haunting
love-sick

ness.

Chung and Ingo *(3)*

a) both apparently

on the winning

side against
cancer though

b) so weakened

that the Corona

virus could e
asily finish–

them-off if
allowed entran

c) ce to their re

establishing

less-protect
ive half-certi

fying future.

Could-have- *(3)*

a) been While wait

ing days even

weeks-on-end
for what most

b) probably wouldn'

t happen does

time-present
become re-rout

ed to nothing
more than a

c) self-establish

ing if possi

bly post–Rank
ean could–

have-been.

The *"pursuit (4)*

a) of happiness"

may have become

for many a
self-determin

b) ing take-it-

while–you–can

most tempting
near–say But

I've discover

c) ed that happi

ness pre-deter
mines its own

route while

d) often leaving

me totally un
prepared for

its encompass
ing resolve.

This mid-March (3)

a) Saturday's

brightened

beyond the
scope of a

b) word-invoking

satisfact

ion Now and
here it speak

s for itself

c) leaving me

but a second
ary self-re

ceptive aware
ness.

Hear-say' (3)

a) s insinuat

ing rumour

s spread
their infect

b) ious design

s quicker

deeper and
even more

thorough
ly-efficient

c) than the Cor

ona virus'

invisible
time-persuas

ions.

The appear (3)

a) ance of a

poetry book

should become
a part of its

b) finalizing

content The

eye may hear
and the ear

may see but
once publish

c) ed such a

book must

speak on its
own thorough

ly poetic–
term

s.

She may have

been the type
who preferred

a childless
marriage be

cause she de
sired her

extra share
of self–in

dulgent pur
posing

s.

He chose his (4)

    a) wife with es

    pecial care

    that she be
    pretty but not

    b) excessive

    ly so contin

    ually desired
    by other men

    that she be
    bright but

    c) not at a

    height above

    his somewhat
    limited resour

    ces At the end

d) his future

wife chose
him more for

intrinsic per
sonal-reason

s.

Fitting a (4)

a) poem just right'

s more like

an aestheti
cally refined

b) woman's dress-

resolve It must

fit but not
too tightly

self-reveal
ing Its color

c) s must match

her own natur

al appearance-
sake And it

should some
how become a

d) part of her

daily self–

feeling's
most–person

al find
s.

Dillon always (4)

a) his grandfather'

s favorite both

distinctly red–
headed certain

b) ing their life

for a higher-

up phase The
one German-Ameri

can still remains in

c) Schwabian home-

towned his
younger admir

er American-

d) Germaned

though ocean
ed apart home-

towned as
well.

The sky' (2)

a) s however hori

zoned claim

s never repet
itously wind–

resolving
even its al

b) *ways a blue*

of now and no–

timed else
sanction

ing depth–
involving

appearance
s.

Trumpism (2)

a) *A president*

incapable

of taking per
sonal responsi

bility for his
own mistakes

b) isn't worthy

character-

wise of the
office he often

uses for such
courageous

decision
s.

For Dillon and (4)

a) a strange time

for a honeymoon

in Europe
when Corona'

b) s spreading

daily and many

nations have
closed their

borders when

c) public trans

portation
's hardly a

safety route
and European

s now in the

d) same category

as dogs closed–
off from the

New World's
freedom–call

s.

Corona (5)

a) Even modern

states of what
ever kind help

less against
this pandemie

b) neither mede

cine's to deal

with it nor a
vaccine to keep

it at door-step'

c) s length Simply

disinfect your
hands (if you'

ve managed to
get the right

d) thing) and keep

your feet safe

ly at home'
s base while

no Boccacio

e) in sight to

entertain its
more sophisti

cated refu
gees.

Awakened (6)

a) with an unsafe

feeling as if

a pogrom in
the offing

b) and no mean

s of self-de

fense left
And that after

the High Court

c) of post-Ausch

witz Germany
had proclaim

ed on Ash Wed
nesday "man"

d) as the measure

of all things

even his own
life and death

when Jesus on

e) that Ash

Wednesday
routed to take-

on our sin-ex

f) posing death

and now re-rout
ing us for a

heavenly fu
ture.

Corona' (7)

a) s the word of

the day the

weeks the mon
ths Though it'

b) s easy to pro

nounce it remain

s invisibly act
ive Though call

ed by name
if doesn't re

c) spond even to

our emergen

cy measure
s It's aloof

and yet thorough
in its aging de

cisive impact

d) churches closed-

down though of

far greater
significance

the important
soccer games

e) either cancelled

or played be

fore a non–exis
tant ghost-like

audience Soon
it won't be

f) possible to

eat–out even

a 2 meters dis
tancing It seem

s that Corona

g) has conquered

our insuffi
cient ineffect

ive defense-
mean

s.

Spring this *(4)*

a) year's rebirth

advertised

so sweetly by
Botticelli

b) seems despite

its usual

ever-change
able appearan

ces even more

c) remote because

of this year'
s constantly

cold-sensed

d) winds and Cor

ona's daily
and last

ing pre-em
inence.

Whatever (2)

> *a) the rules may*
>
> have been
>
> even establish
> ed long
>
> ago He'll
> make his own
>
>
> *b) to enable a*
>
> fluency of
>
> his especial
> ly express
>
> ive word–de
> pendent
>
> mean
> s.

Corona and (3)

> *a) Trump opposite*
>
> sides of the
>
> same coin
> minted at

b) some secret

ly invisible

place of their
own self-satis

fying choice
Always in effect

c) tive use spon

taneously

signifying
a self-warrant

ed cause.

Exceptional (3)

a) situation

s A life with

out exception
al situation

b) s is hard to

image as a

life at all
Every day may

deviate from

c) what we've

tried to ex
ample for

our own daily
routine

s.

Some zoo- (3)

a) animals behave

as if they're

on display for
us Others seem

to take us

b) for what should

have been cag
ed-in as

well as if the
zoo wasn't just

a kind of an

c) imal park but

a human one
for our strange

ly voiced and
clothed appear

ance
s.

Do we make (2)

a) history or

does history

reconceive
us The case

of the con
tinually other

b) wiseness of once

communistic

East Germany seem
s like a prior

ity example
of the ladder.

Small talk'

s as much a
waste of time

as never ask
ing the most

timely relev
ant-question

s as if life'
s incapable

of answer
ing-back.

Why (3)

a) do we

in the West
refer to what'

s confused con
fusing… when

Confucious

b) himself was

a highly order
ed rational

and ethical
thinker of

first-rate

c) quality

and his ideas
still remain

important e
ven in today'

s China.

Half-mooned (2)

a) At 6 am while

only half-a

moon cut
right-down-

the-middle
seemed to

b) mirror my

own state-of-

being incom
plete but to

what extent
and why now.

Rosemarie' (5)

a) s birthday bet

ween the Ides

of March and
the Vernal E

b) quinox desig

nating my own

identity–
cause the

death of a
once-upon-a

c) time lonesome

self now re

birthed in
the spring

time's awaken
ing love-call

d) s Has Ingo

once again

become rerout
ed from death'

s apparently
time-adept

e) impenetrable

cause to

signs of a
reawakening

life-bespok
en triumph.

Each tree (2)

a) now in early

spring seem
s to have
chosen its

own dressed
apparent-color

b) s not for

public-display

but more of
a self-aspir

ing identity-
cause.

Frame-of-re (2)

a) ference Family

has become

for many more
like a frame-

of-reference
as books once

b) fully partici

pating but

now shelved
for a possi

ble time-at
tending re

read.

7 am and this *(7)*

a) once half-flour

ishing self-de
termining

b) moon seems to

be fading-out

Have I become
partly respon

sible for writ

c) ing-it-through

from a once
cherished

but now un
seen anonymous

appearance

d) Looking-back

in retrospect

I begin to
realize that

some once
half-friend

e) ship person

s seem as that

7 am moon to
have slowly fa

ded–out not
even revived

f) for a self-

standing most-

personal un
timely-reappear

ance.

Who's living (5)

a) in that top-

storied house

right across
the way I think

b) it may be a

Syrian or other

wise Moslem
capable of ex

porting that
Near Eastern

c) conflict right

to our over–

sized Tom cat
occasional

ly inhabiting
door–step It

d) may be a part

of my Jewish

historical
background

that makes
me as my once

e) ghetto-inhabit

ing grandmoth

er particul
arly fearful

of what'
s -to-come.

Each day (3)

 a) that Corona

 virus seem

 s to be
 creeping–in

 b) on us until

 as in Italy

 the hardest
 hit there'

 s no place
 to go but

 c) home-sitt

 ing as if

 waiting for
 death's unan

 nounced call
 ing

 s.

Now Eliot' (4)

    a) s "April's

    the cruellest

    month" though
    a half-month

    b) earlier seem

    s to actual

    ize Botticelli'
    s sweetness

    with the cruel

    c) crucifying

    death of Jesus
    as if that e

    mancipating

d) blood had be

come the e
ternal spring'

s real-flower
ings.

Target-range (3)

a) Can we simply

seal–death–off

from our own
life-pursuing

b) aims keeping

it on the

outside of our
indwelling

ambition
s Or has it

c) from the very

beginning

kept us with
in its own

target–range.

The first (4)

a) Sars virus high

ly lethal 30%

dead but not
very contagious

b) whereas Corona

seems opposite

ly-sourced
hardly lethal

but highly con
tagious And if

c) we're as usual

unprepared may

be the next in
visible one will

be both highly
lethal and ex

d) tremely conta

gious and we'll

be left with
the ruins of a

once florish
ing-civilizat

ion.

Exampled *(4)*

a) China availed

the resource

s of an author
itarian re

b) gime to exam

ple its effi

ciency again
st Corona

While Trump

c) in the guise

of robber–capi
talism would

have transplan
ted an entire

d) German head-

start viral

team to the
credit of Amer

ica–first.

An incompleted (7)

a) summing-up

First he left

the Kurds our
best fighter

b) s against Isis

to the destruct

ive whims of
their Turkish

enemies Then he

c) allowed Isis

to bomb the
Saudi's oil

fields without
the most-necess

d) ary American-

response And now

he's resorting
to robber–capit

alism to save

e) the America-

first image a
gainst Corona

Have we ever
had such a

f) character

less president
still capable

of courageous

g) help for un

born children
and for God'

s Chosen Peo
ple.

This is per (5)

    a) haps the time

    to touch these

    smallest of
    spring grass

    b) ed-flower

    s to their

    newly color
    ed most inno

    cent of claim

c) s to let the

brightening
sun vanguish

our daily Cor
ona fears

d) to thank The

Good Lord for

whatever love
He's expended

e) on those of

us unworthy

of His so un
limited forgive

ness.

Only the grand (9)

    a) parents We're

    only the grand

    parents at not
    only a geographi

    b) ical distance

    but from the

    beginning
    somehow as for

    eign to our
    grandchildren

    c) as we've be

    come for our

    American re
    latives We set

    the example
    and they've ta

d) ken it for

their own good

Afterall we're
only the grand

parent

e) s For Andreas

we're in the
highest risk-

group over 80
and not so ro

f) bust as Neil

would have it

The Italian
s hardest hit

European

g) s daily mourn

their disease
-stricken

grandparent
s If infect

h) ed would there

really be no

hospital bed
left for us

and would we

i) still be re

member
ed by our

so distant
grandchild

ren.

Easiest to (4)

    a) call- off the

    dentist My

    teeth however
    badly resolv

    b) ed will have

    to manage on–

    their–own for
    the weeks–to–

    come Yes that

    c) tooth-smile

    of mine will
    have to re

    main unrecon

    d) ciled with

    the somewhat
    inflated cost

    s of dental–
    care.

Once the trad (5)

    a) ional rhyme

    meter and pre-

    establish
    ing forms have

    become dis
    carded what re

    b) mains "poetic"

    even in the

    modern sensed–
    words rebirth

    ed to their
    once mint-value

    c) claim You

    may see it

    your way
    perspectiv

    ed through
    use and famil

d) iarly cherish

ed insight

s whereas what
the poet envis

ions remains
word-perspect

e) ived by a dia

logued re

conciling other
wise meaning

ed self-compo
sure.

Is this new *(6)*

a) Corona virus

simply speed

ing-up the
generation'

b) s replacement-

cycle The older

die perhaps at
a quicker and

not so pleas

c) ing pace the

younger take-
over what's

no longer so
effectively

d) left-behind

Why then this

fear of what'
s ultimately

a natural
process or

e) does this

natural pro

cess preclude
the Judaic–

Christian also
democratical

f) ly self-mean

ingful individ

ually–personal
life–signifi

cance.

The great *(4)*

a) month-long al

most invincible

Australian
fires left

b) millions of

an otherwise

animal life
as a flamed

sacrificial–

c) offering much

as the equal
ly helpless

Jewish offer

d) ing daily per

petuated at
those diverse

ly centered
death-camp

s.

A question (7)

    a) able ownership

    Trying to read

    this one or
    perhaps that

    b) poem through

    the sensibil

    ity of this
    friend or that

    one's special

    c) ly expressed

    thematic–
    affinity

    Does that
    poem become

d) more their

s than my

own as Neil'
s acute and

accurate re

e) membrance

s of what I'
d long-since

forgotten
or the long–

f) dead Charles

Seliger's

finely-con
ceived paint

g) ings hanging

now in the

living room
of an unknown

recipient.

To celebrate (4)

a) life as an in

tricate part

of one's own
receptive

b) sensibility

reveals a

creational
religious

ity which

c) Jesus made His

own by pre-re
surrecting

his ardent if

d) oft wrongly path

ed follower
s with a fu

tured hopeful
ness.

Is this now (2)

a) daily bright

ly apparent–

spring but a
self-decept

ive means of

b) disguising

the Corona
virus' omin

ous secretly
on–going pro

ceeding
s.

Are works- (2)

a) of-art espec

ially meant

for those
who feel their

own aesthetic
equally es

b) poused or for

those who

feel in them
selves a pre

viously un
touched- express

iveness.

American presi (3)

a) dents are oath

ed-in with one

hand on the
bible and a

b) fully mouthed

promise to do

what's in the
interests of

the country's

c) (not the world'

s) interest
s Trump at least

read-this-one-
right.

Patches of (3)

    a) flowers in an

    otherwise

    more or less
    barren land

    scape as here

    b) and there bloss

    oming trees
    colored through

    an appreciat
    ive hand–touch

    ed reach All

    c) this as but a

    start of an
    as yet incomplet

    ed work–defin
    ing familiar

    ity.

Poland still (3)

a) tracked with the

routes of Jew

ish suffering
but now other

b) wise exampled

restaurant

s closed chur
ches open for

the faithful

c) s protective

prayers again
st a now in

visible but
still danger

ous enemy.

Donatello

You can't

look away
from a Dona

tello statue
It places you

right there
where he want

s you to dia
logue his vision

ary self-asser
tive phrasing

s.

March 18 (4)

a) Rosemarie'

s birthday

seems to be
growing into

b) itself as this

sun–expectant

day as Rose
marie once

from childhood
to womanly

c) sourced (if one

considers such

time-zone
s) She's (I'm

quite certain)
much the same

d) person even

after 59 year

s of a
so love-accomo

dating out-of-
bounds marr

iage.

How's to ex *(9)*

a) plain that most

ly ex-Nazis

rebuilt a now
democratic

b) German nation

Most of them

neither Nazis
nor Democrat

s but the type
always ready

c) to sail the

best boat a

vailable to
the nearest

time-securing
port Home fam

d) ily the oppor

tunist's

most desirable
life's daily

pursuing-value.

e) I'll serve

the state the
king I'll serve

the church the
pope for many

interchange
able possibili

f) ties Not only

the cameleon

s capable of
daily color–

change

g) s That mediev

al well remain
ed too deep to

source its
bottomed-down

h) self We threw

stones in

to its echoing
watering-depth

perhaps not
realizing

i) we were test

ing-out our

walled-in
protective

identity-
cause.

"Don't be a (11)

a) fraid" they

kept repeat

ing But after
they'd outlaw

b) ed most every

aspect of our

daily life
leaving the

streets all–
but–empty and

c) every possible

amusement for

bidden Did they
really expect

we'd just sit
at home daily

d) and fearless

ly listening

to their life–
limiting ad

vice It's usual

e) ly easier to

defend one
self against a

visible enemy
than an invis

f) ible one Satan

we can hardly

kill as he
keeps snake-

like chang
ing forms So

g) we've given him

horns a tail

and other
strangely un

familiar attri
butes to enable

h) us to end his

terrifying

domain The
Coronas will

come and go

i) leaving death

and suffering
behind But

there's only
one invisible

j) source that re

mains through

His blood nail
ed wounds ca

pable of re

k) deeming us

even from our
own invisibly

depthed sin
ful-being.

My mother (8)

a) (God bless her

for the love

she gave me
as a child)

b) remained a

modest very

helpful and
highly athlet

ic country–

c) club-girl in

to her ever–
aging year

s I'll always
s associate

d) her with one

of her favor

ite song "The
Queen of May"

That defined
her very-be

e) ing to its

very last

ing syllable
My father

(really a good
and kindly man

f) at heart) in

his most ex

pansive moment
s intuned his

"There's a
long long trail

g) awinding into

the land of my

dreams …" It
became his life

fathomed even

h) beyond his mytholog

ically indwell
ing aspirat

ions.

Could he re

    cognize his
    own voice e

    choing through
    the sea's

    time-immens
    ing continu

    ity.

This spring

    continually
    reminds me of

    a young lady
    not yet fully

    aware of her
    own self-ex

    tending tonal
    ity.

For a creat (2)

    a) ive artist

    his education

    formal or
    better-still

    self-learned
    may become

b) applied as

an image–en

dowed compara
tively–adept

self–imagin
ing.

What Luther (4)

a) fully realized

the need for

a direct con
frontation

b) with the bibli

cal word with

out the burden
of unnecessary

intermediarie

c) s Serious art of

whatever kind de
mands a similar

"I and thou"

d) confrontat

ional but

still complement
ary response.

These long (2)

    a) nakedly aspiring

    trees now cloth

    ed in varied
    pre-establish

    ing colors as

b) the self-perpet

uating gladness
of little girl

s dressed in
their appreciat

ive smile
s.

Those artist (3)

a) s obsessed with

the desire

for fame
should learn

from the Cor

b) ona virus now

spreading
its invisible

allure through
out the entire

world independ

c) ent of age

race gender
and religion

its world–
unifying unseen

death–envelop
ing display.

Is Donatello' *(5)*

a) s art inherent

in the means

of its dialog
uing form–in

b) habiting ex

pressive

ness whether
of marble

Ghiberti

c) bronze … Or

is he trying
to penetrate

the pre-deter
mining source of

his mainly re

d) ligious figure

s or ultimate
ly inspired by

his own personal
raison d'être

Is he a Christ

e) ian or classi

cal artist
or somehow a

time-availing
synthesis

of both.

The chaste

> and so child-
> like innocen
>
> ce of these
> early spring
>
> buds when fall
> en leave scarce
>
> ly a reminder
> of blood-touch
>
> ed impression
> s.

Trump's "A (5)

> *a) merica first"*
>
> 's really noth
>
> ing other than De
> Gaulle ism
>
>
> *b) Both accept*
>
> their nation
>
> al accents for
> other nation
>
> s as well al
> though DeGaulle

c) was then weak

ly-sourced where

as Trump know
s full-well the

power of the
American presi

d) dency When it'

s a question

of money or
now of life

and death one
realizes that

e) a truly United Eur

ope's but un

realistic
wishful-think

ing.

Rosemarie' (4)

> *a) s so-called*
>
> "old age"'
>
> s beautifying
> presence
>
> *b) has made me*
>
> daily once a
>
> gain aware
> that sculpture
>
> such as Dona
>
> *c) tello's doesn't*
>
> lose its effi
> cient self–re
>
> vealing know–

d) how even when

exposed to
times of more

than visual–
use.

Flooded with (3)

a) light and the

warmth of a

pre–establish
ing spring–

b) time what could

be more welcome

than this while
the invisible

Corona Virus'

c) spreading its

diseased tenta
cled reach to

those unseen
realms of our

daily endanger
ed presence.

Comparison' (4)

a) s rarely encom

pass more than

a dissembling
likeness All

b) that's created

remains unique

ly sourced e
ven one-egged

twins Yet many
of us tend to

c) think and sense

in comparative

terms as a
means of better

realizing this
or even that

d) or most likely

our own need

for a safely
securing home-

sake.

Those little

girl imitation
s of their

mother's oft
visible mood–

spells more
than simply

a develop
mental phase?

A dangerous (4)

a) comparison when

Chancellor Merkel

underlines the
importance of a

b) Corona-together

ness "more necess

ary than at any
time since the

2nd World War"

c) I can hardly i

magine that such
a together

ness in Hitler'
s destructive

d) and self-destruct

ive Germany would

be characteriz
ed for Merkel as

well as essent
ially-positive.

Corona's keep (3)

    a) ing the dogs

    on the street

    while other
    humans not allow

    b) ed It's neverthe

    less "a dog's

    life" because
    their freedom'

    s the only way

    c) out leaving them

    over-walked ex
    hausted in need

    of improved
    safety-measure

    s.

There's not (3)

a) death in the

air but death

in your mind
It remain

s there in

b) active but

still poised
for the new

est statistic
s It activate

s its own

c) fears invade

s your dream
s with the

helpless feel
of a coming

all–impend
ing loss.

If a poem (2)

a) remains some

thing special

does its value
deprectiate

b) when it's be

come so numer

ously–birthed
so commonly–

expressed or

c) does each poem

deserve a spec
ially–worded

message–of–
its–own.

No it's not (3)

a) like those trans

ported to the

death camp
s few will

b) die of Corona

far fewer than

the 97 % who didn't
survive the camp

s But it's
still a most

c) necessary re

minder this
spring time that

life and death
have always re

mained inti
mately-sourc

ed.

Why does it *(3)*

a) become necess

ary to defend

our heritage
whether Ger

man Jewish or

b) Spanish …

Severe fail
ings document

our always-re
levant-past

but if we're

c) believer

s then forgive
ness should

accompany
a daily

life-renewal.

Franz our (3)

   a) littlest neigh

   bor of almost

   four become
   s daily propell

   b) ed with such a

   life-renewing

   vitality that
   I myself be

   come age-divid
   ed with his

   c) exuberance

   but with a

   more-lasting-
   feeling of

   times-long-
   since-past.

In the course (4)

    a) of time I've

developed a

strong distaste
for such word

    b) s as "of course"

or "naturally"

They're a mean
s of presenting

very personal o

    c) pinions as some

how authoritat
ive I prefer

"seems" or "per

d) haps" as a lessen

ing-down of my
own self-securing

subjectiv
ity.

This morn (3)

a) ing it seem

s as if I'

ve been bloss
omed into

b) these tree

's expendible

whiteness
not that of

wisdomed–
hair but more

c) like a contin

uity of out

spreading re
ceptive–glad

nesses.

No one for (2)

a) got Rosemarie’

s birthday

this year (as
if they ever

did) She’s been
phoned carded

b) gifted into

the fully re

ceptive but
always self–

shadowing
times–to–

come.

Corona' (4)

a) s been signi

ficiently
crowned with

self-import

b) ance though

less deadly
than many of

her forebear
ers she re

mains contag

c) iously prolif

ic with a

world-wide
reputation

as a spoiler
of whatever

d) and where

ever our once

activating
free-timed

pleasure
s.

When I first (5)

a) contemplate

the lawn strewn

with the al
most four-year-

b) old Franz's

toys my first

impression
he's living–

out a fullness

c) of our almost

unlimiting-
times But then

I begin to
question

whether too–

d) much doesn't

lessen a person
alized imagina

tion But then
this propell

ing Franz'

e) s too-much

himself (or
so it seem

s) to ever
stop-short.

Even the e (2)

a) ver-daily can

become poeti

zed depend
ing on that

particular

b) perspective

and a word–
sense to match

its dialogu
ing raison d'

être.

However self- *(5)*

   a) rewarding it

   may feel to

   live-out-to-
   the-fullest

   b) one's especial

   ly pre-given

   gifts (aren'
   t I doing ex

   actly that with
   this prolific-

   c) poetizing)

   Yet Aron's

   sport's abilit
   ies if so fully

   out-lived with
   the necessary

d) holding-back

reserves lead

s to chronical
ly-injured

e) and that's

self-destruct
ive of his

future goal
s.

Why write a (3)

a) bout poetry

(as I've been

so often ask
ed) when one

b) can poem-it-

directly

Prose remain
s a lesser ex

pressive–form
because good

c) poetry says-it-

more and deep

er through its
fundamental

word–control.

Learning better (3)

    a) Most difficult

when one's been

quoted against
oneself – only

    b) a very persist

ent listener

can become a
ware of such

a contradict
ion while the

    c) answer's remain

ed unchanged

"I've learned
better since

then."

Surrendered! (9)

    a) Have we surren

    dered to this

    invisible
    virus Every

    b) thing's closed

    down no concert

    s theater movie
    s We can't even

    eat–out visit

    c) friends It seem

    s as if it'
    s set the

    terms No plea
    sures now or

d) he'll close the

hospitals over

filled as the
graveyard

s There's a

e) no-ways-out

the border
s have been

closed Surren
dered it's set

the terms

f) Has it triumph

ed because man'
s become his

own and only
master over

birth identity

g) love and death

Has the invis
ible Satan now

laid claim
s to our very–

h) being As long

as there's a

defense an an
swer as long

as we've a
faith in a

i) Higher Being

there's still

a lingering
hope He'll once

again save-us-
from-ourselv

es.

Don't continu (10)

    a) ally ask of

    motives better

    to concentrate
    on the fact

    b) s themselves

    s Yes we Ameri

    cans needed the
    defeated German

    s against the

    c) Russian Commun

    ist threat After
    Auschwitz and

    a merciless war
    they didn't de

    d) serve anything

    better than the

    Morgenthau Plan
    Instead our

    soldiers fed

e) their children

with candie
s Don't ask

why they tast
ed so sweet

f) Our neighbor

s feeding

their penned-
in chicken

s until they'

g) re fat enough

juicy enough
to be eaten

Chickens don'

h) t ask why they'

re being fed
nor do we quest

ion their tasty
remain

i) s poetry as all

genuine art's
a revealing

of another per
spective on

life it's natur

j) al beauty it's

inbespoken
need to depth

our otherwise
timely recept

ive-calling
s.

Doing his (2)

    a) daily round

    s so softly

    as an angel
    treading on

    clouds per

    b) haps because

    he'd been siz
    ed at such

    a height of
    distancing-

    sound
    s.

On this (4)

    a) "World sparrow

    day" so small-

    minded I didn'
    t believe it

b) at first an en

dangered spec

ies though they'
re everywhere

know all the
tricks of that

c) after-meal ap

proach "Seeing'
s believing it

if that's an
endanger

ed specie

d) s I may

need to re
write my own

sense of such
a world–wide

urgency.

Not every (5)

a) cough's a Cor

ona–cough

Not every fe
ver's Corona–

b) based Corona

monopolize

s our new
s as well Bavar

ian German Euro

c) pean Corona

news … Few
seem to have

become aware
of spring's

d) blossoming

promises or

the grasses'
newly flavoured

e) coloring

s or of the

many Franz'
s world-wide

discovierie
s.

We've be *(4)*

a) come an espec

ially protect

ed species
Those over 80

b) also weaken

ed by other health

problems We
need to be

specially
taken–care–

c) of as mother'

s wheeling a

long their
youngest spross

I find
myself measur

d) ing that self–

inhabiting en

fant with my
own bodily–se

cured dimens
ions.

"It's never (5)

   a) too late to

   find a mate"
   My 100–plus
   mother an es

   b) pecially gift

   ed marriage–

   broker special
   ized in that

   younger genera

   c) tion of 75-and-

   over though she

   never herself
   considered such

   a marriage–leap

d) (My father weigh

ed too heavily

on her George-
time memorable

past) while she
herself a rout

e) ined marriage-

broker rarely

if ever took
"no" for a final

answer.

A package-deal? (4)

a)No Jaffin's

not really a

package-deal
Some like this

b) others that

Yes I some

times feel like
Rosemarie's

mother who need

c) ed at least

4 suitcase
s for her

timely–vacat
ions While I'

m not yet quite

d) certain how

many empty one
s are still

waiting to be
packed.

Curfew (5)

a) starting to

day with no

one (health and
private-supply ex

b) ception

s) allowed

out of house
and home

For some work

c) ing people o

vercome with
a strange

feeling of "I
didn't really

d) ask for this"

and for their

home-bound
spouses "I was

just getting
used to him"

e) (or her) at

the most necess
ary time-length

s "And they
lived happily-

ever-after".

Those retire (5)

a) d more easily

confuse the

days of the
week while

b) for some like

myself free-

time Saturday
s seem to in

habit more

c) than their

weekly (d)reserv
ed stop-over

s The time
s we've set

d) and ordered

remain artifi

cial but time
itself take

s little in
terest in man'

e) s attempt at

naming its e

ver-recurring
steadfast

ness.

Once again (4)

a) on a cool

and rainy Satur

day morning
He remained

b) completely-

at-odds with

his own thor
oughly-sanct

ioned-misbehav

c) ior even fear

ing he might
have endanger

ed their ear

d) ly spring-budd

ing friend
ship now most

decidedly off–
course.

Off-track (2)

a) We often feel

others will

react much the
same way as

we but such
assumption

b) s usually re

main off-track

while we often
misjudge our

own intuitive
ly spontane

ous-response.

Are these re *(2)*

a) curring rain

s perhaps

listening
to their own

echoing aware
ness of a

b) continuous

ly rhythmic

and repetit
ively reviving

self-certain
ty.

When at 15 (2)

a) I started to

write it was

not so much
what I want

ed to say but

b) the as yet

unrealized
word–cleans

ing way of
saying–it

just–right.

My father (3)

a) needed to win

at whatever or

whomever That
was simply his

b) way of doing

things most

often perhap
s to impress

his once ghett
oed father'

c) s almost un

limited reserv

es for such
receptive

ly encompass
ing success-

storie
s.

Despite

> these continu
> ously oncoming
>
> rains these
> blossoming
>
> colors haven'
> t been washed-
>
> out of my
> mind's light-re
>
> trieving time-
> set.

The father (4)

> *a) fat and jovial*
>
> his promiscu
>
> ous wife and
> daughter

b) s otherwise

self–satisfy

ing He daily
at Wall Street

where he made

c) and left million

s for his three
"ladies" After

his will many

d) stopped think

ing of him as
"the nothing"

he'd really be
come.

Not now to (4)

> *a) aim high*
>
> where the cloud
> s extend
> their heaven
>
>
> *b) ly ever-change*
>
> able reach but
>
> to set–down
> low where the
>
> greened grass
>
>
> *c) es evoke the*
>
> smallest of
> their flowering
>
> instincts The

d) poet should teach

us anew to per
ceive these fin

est of timely-
perspective

s.

Corona-Munich (2)

a) lonely empty

streets as New

York after The
Great Blizzard

of '47 a hushed

b) silence that

prevaded what
ever could

still remain
listening-a

loud.

It snowed (2)

> *a) the night*
> through releas
> ing its self–
> exposing sad
> nesses felt–

> *b) down to his un*
> touchable
> and continual
> ly forgot
> en dream–
> flow.

In the dark *(3)*

a) of winter's un

expected return

leaving spring'
s multi–color

b) ed flower

s totally un

prepared now
hidden below

the snow–en

c) closure

s of a momen
tary self–for

getful
ness.

On the scent (5)

a) Hunters Brueghel-

like on the

scent dogs–
down for its

fresh-blood-im

b) pression

s in snow in
to the wood

s of its once
protective–

c) silence

s Aren't

poems to be
described

in much-the–

d) same-way their

scent the pre-
evocative

call to foll

e) ow into the

darkness of
unremember

ed dream
s.

Theme and *(3)*

a) Variation

s With so

much to re
cord and such

b) a vast express

ive need Theme

and variation
s as "Thirteen

ways" seems

c) the most pre

sentable
means for a

word-desir
ing impact.

At least (2)

a) it's adorned

with the same

purifying
coloring

s openly–
white tree

b) buds and the

domesticat

ing snow
now seeming

ly settl
ed-down

home-bred.

We Rosemarie (4)

a) and myself

high-risk

openly expos
ed time-bomb

b) s confined to

house and gard

en only such as
dog-walks

allowed out

c) I mean we so-

called old and
feeble seem to

have been es

d) pecially mark

ed-off for
the omnipot

ent Corona
virus.

Otherwised (3)

a) The comfort

able blue of
a late winter

ed morning

b) and these drift

ing-white
clouds seem to

be expanding
time's light–

c) securing hold

a panorama

of an other
wise than Cor

ona-perspect
ive.

Sunday (3)

a) all the church

es closed–down
Corona's per
spective seem

s here suffi

b) ciently up-to-

date agnostic
ally–modern

Let all the
church bell

s ring if

c) they like but

for emptied
soul–reaching

scarcely sha
dowing church–

benches.

My 17-year- *(3)*

a) old thrill of

Playland's
down–surging

b) roller-coas

ter's that

lifted me back
once again to

life's more con

c) sistently re

warding if less
stimulat

ing pleasur
ings.

For Hanni (3)

a) Does so-call

ed "Mother

Earth" exer
cise a–will–

b) of-its-own

or has it

been so crea
ted to deny

in its own

c) pre-given way

its misused by
man's God–cho

sen over-seer
s.

Routine' (4)

    a) s love's daily

    used–down dan

    ger I'll do
    that for

    b) you'll do that

    for me as if

    marriage had
    become a role-

    play of inter

    c) changeable

    time–afford
    ing effort
    s If continu

d) ally genuine

ly affection-sourc
ed-love can't

stand-on-it
own what can.

So quickly (2)

a) the snow's melt

ed away as

those some
time's darkly-

sensed-feel
ings while the

b) uprising sun'

s so bright

ly intensed
its own pre

valent-sur
facing

s.

Dreamed-reali (5)

    a) ties began to

    merge into

    his daily
    chores that

    b) he couldn't

    be certain

    of having
    done or

    "only" dreamed

    c) of his setting

    the morning'
    s breakfast

    table Upon
    thorough in

d) spection he

hadn't so he

repeated his
"only" dreamed-

purposing
s Do such

e) dreamed-reali

ties still re

tain a cert
tain effective

meaning of
their own.

He'd seen it (4)

a) all before Some

poets would per

haps tire of
the same daily

b) windowed-view

I don't because

I'm not quite
the same daily

person while

c) writing-it-out

that's proof
enough that

the "same"
view has ta

d) ken-on another

not so samed

perspect
ive for this

daily other
wise–poet.

Even if (5)

    a) time remain

    s continual

    ly the same
    as the sett

    b) ing for a

    Shakespeare-

    like theater
    It's been set

    not for its

    c) own sake but

    for live act
    ors who might

    re-time their
    life-appearan

d) ces playing

the diverse

parts of a
character–

full change
ability Aren'

e) t we also other

wise with each

unwary person
who happens to

come our cha
melion–like

way.

Each Shakes (4)

a) pearean charact

er so differen

ciated because
their timed–ex

b) perience help

s pre-determine

their always
changeable

nature whereas

c) the ancient

Greek character

izations as
those of Sopho

cles remain

d) always samed

statically-im
pending for

their oncom
ing-fall.

If a single (4)

> *a) simple virus*
>
> substancial
>
> ly named "Cor
> ona" can effect
>
>
> *b) the life of*
>
> most everyone
>
> here on earth
> under its time
>
> ly-crowned but
> invisible ap
>
>
> *c) pearance must*
>
> we if possible
>
> remain prepared
> for what's outside
>
> our own control
> but may be
>
>
> *d) caused by our*
>
> own presump
>
> tive self-ele
> vating behav
>
> ior.

Their "true (3)

    a) nature" Some per

    sons hide their

    "true nature"
    for appear

    b) ance-sake of

    clothes fancy

    cars even univer
    sity degree

    s speaking
    for themselve

    c) s but perhap

    s only attri

    butes of such
    self-forsaken

    ing person
    s.

"It's what (5)

    a) it means for

    me" whether

    a biblical
    text or a

    b) piece of classi

    cal music …

    But it may
    have meant

    something

    c) very differ

    ent for the
    creator often

    doesn't know
    what it actual

    ly means being

d) too involved

in the dialogi
cal intuitive

process itself
Meaning takes–

on its own

e) sense-of-pur

pose often e
lusively

self–involv
ing.

How bright

can cold be
come on this

late winter
ed day quest

ioning the
hard–shine of

its own untime
ly self–secur

ing identity–
claim

s.

Rosemarie may (2)

> *a) have just turn*
>
> ed 82 but she'
>
> s turned-back
> that beauty
>
> length to suit
> her nicely blue
>
>
> *b) but not yet*
>
> fully lengthen
>
> ed newly-sty
> led morning'
>
> s accomodat
> ions.

Many of those (3)

> *a) who play the*
>
> money-game
>
> have lost out
> at that loved-

b) one Our class

mate Schlesing

er now worth
several million

four-timed di

c) vorced perhaps

because money-
mindedness

blinded him to
the lasting

d) value of that

otherwise

femininely re
ceptive-compan

ionship.

Sculpture (4)

a) even of the

finest kind

with all of
its physical

b) ly evocative

tactile-value

s missing some
thing essential

for me that meta

c) physically

spaced sense of
an untouch

able distant
ly focused–a

d) *wareness also*

the poetic

transparen
cies of say

post–1850
Corot.

A young child' (3)

a) s measuring

the unspoken

boundarie
s of his own

b) time-availing

world's really

no different
from the poet'

s dialoguing

c) anew whatever

seems at least
to be engag

ingly looking–
back.

He didn't (3)

a) stick to the

rules–of–the–

game a reason
ably short poet

b) ry book every

3 years or so

while it kept
writing him

more–further
into those

c) silently a

waiting place

s for a poeti
cally cultivat

ed–arrival.

It's like (3)

a) discovering

an alternate

reading for
some of Li

b) Shang yin'

s more her

metic poem
s Which way

did he mean
it and which not

c) Poems that

leave one quest
ioning remain

better suited
for future read

ings?

When even (3)

    a) after some 59

    years the meet

    ing of eyes
    can still melt–

    b) down whatever

    accumulating

    distances
    have occurred

    and the embra
    cing of hand

    c) s can re-es

    tablish a

    unity for
    purposing the

    future togeth
    erness.

Those child (4)

a) transports the

parents left

behind to the
"final solut

ion" Their child

b) dren growthed in a

strange country
with a strange

language and
parents of a

foreign breed

c) ing repeating it

self here and
now in Germany

with the parent
less children

survivors of

d) that endless

war in Syria
without even a

self-sufficient
identity-claim.

With Corona (4)

a) daily feeding

on a now clos

ed-down once
socially-orien

b) ted-society

and a dear

friend plagu
ed with cancer'

s (last)ing
phase pained to

c) the very depth

of his very-be

ing with our no-
way-out perhap

s even to his
coming funeral

d) Corona crown

ed with her

self-satisfy
ing satanical

ly destruct
ive imperson

al triumph!

At least act (8)

a) ually at most

we have each
other a love–
blend that has

b) held and deep

ened through

the years
But what of

friends left

c) alone with

little or no
personal con

tact allowed
as long as

d) Corona's deny

ing their

existencial
social need

s These high–

e) flying bird-

flight's sha
dowing the

heavens
with their

f) daily earthly

needs while
here our

ground-based
airports all

g) but complete

ly shut-down

little or no
contacts out

side the famil
iar family-

h) base when glob

alization'

s become our
most persist

ent future-
calling.

Why that (2)

a) time-repeat

ing image of

Jack Sadowsky
our summer

camp's most
active fisher

b) man plying

those deeply

darkened wa
ters with his

if less self-
confiding ex

pectation
s.

As long as (5)

a) this curfew'

s reducing

each day to
a repetitive-

b) sameness as

if time's still

incapable of
repeating it

self while

c) these pre-

determin
ing poems tak

ing little or
no notice of

d) what's allow

ed and what'

s not keep in
habiting my

poetry pad

e) with their

newly discov

ered long–as
piring in

sight
s.

No scholar *(3)*

a) comes to work

with a blank–

page in mind –
No difference

b) here from the

endeavouring

poet Because
either before

or during his
scholarly

c) training he'

s become in

habited with
what one might

call a sublim
inal-bias.

These indig *(2)*

a) enous trees

keep growing

leaving be
hind all those

people-bound
earthly pro

b) blems until

they've reach

ed the necess
ary height

for a bird–
watching wit

nessing.

The usual (5)

a) way's for u

sual people

offering a
protective

b) familiar

ity for diffi

cult time
s and what

times aren't

c) difficult

The unusual
's often boat

ed alone in a
wide expanse

d) of waters with

out clearly

marked-off ex
tending boundar

ies they'll have

e) to discover

personally
for their still

home-shored
possibilit

ies.

"New born" (3)

    a) my Nicodemus

    Christening–

    text meant
    for me not

    b) that I'd be

    come a better

    ed person while
    offering a

    new life–en
    dowing perspect

    c) ive a firm

    ly establish

    ed Christ–bible–
    faith–love orien

    tation.

My short (2)

    a) list of good

    friends once

    again shorten
    ing down to

    a death-con
    suming yet

    b) still time-ex

    tending awaken

    ed even dream
    ed through re

    membran
    ces.

Two-faced (5)

    a) Rosemarie

    realizing

    those few
    old-time

b) houses here

and nearby as

a part of
her youthful

remembran

c) ces so that

each one torn-
down leaves

something
empty not

d) only there

but in her

heart–length
as well Those

houses of the
late 30s aspir

ing an innocent
ly adept image

of a society a

e) bout to embark

on a devastat
ing war and

a Jew-free
Germany.

Don't read (2)

a) it but write

it Input and

output now
levelling–

out to a

b) sculptural

ly redefining

of an
eye-balanc

ing together
ness.

She's become

> closest of all
> that I've known
>
> or shall ever
> possibly know
>
> to a Walt Whit
> manesque self–
>
> adorning pedes
> talled prevail
>
> ing-likeness.

Why do reflec (2)

> *a) tions of even*
>
> the most color
>
> fully delight
> ful present
>
> able flowering
> branches al
>
>
> *b) ways remain*
>
> neither soft
>
> er nor sweet
> er than color
>
> less self-impend
> ing shadow
>
> ings.

Partnerships (6)

a) 82 seems to

be the most
common age

to die of
this Corona

b) virus We sen

iors become

crowned with
death's appar

ent need for
life-experien

c) ed if unequal

led partner

s My father a
first-class

money-raiser

d) maintained

he'd entered
a partnership

with The Living
God He provided

the necessary

e) funds for the

weak and needy
and The Good

Lord would re
spond with even

more than

f) just His re

ciprocat
ing loving–

kindness.

After the (3)

a) *strict Bavar*

ian shut-down

of most
everything

b) *except life-*

preserving

measure
s Rosemarie

and I began
to feel much

c) *like those pre*

serves stored

in the cellar
for eventual

times-of-cri
sis.

Bird-talk *(5)*

a) black bird

with tiny
though acti

b) vating eye

s just land
ed on my wood

en balcony
for a short–

c) time-breath

er or perhap

s a somewhat
extended sun–

bath turned

d) his question

ing tiny eye
s in my dir

ection as if
to say "I've

e) learned to

fly but it'

s never-too-
late."

This late- *(5)*

a) time Polonius

provoking

ly observed
whether we

b) like it or

not we've all

become opport
unists trying

to keep our

c) heads above wa

ter when those
high tides come

rolling-in
But the guilty

d) moon despite

our apparent

foot–hold
there keep

s purposing

e) its under-hand

ed if at time
s catastroph

ic endevour
ings.

Poem-titles (2)

a) Yes poem-title

s seem to at

least direct
ion the oft

unexpectant

b) reader in its

own exclus
ive though

oft ambiguous
ly word–prom

pting design
s.

Disoriented (9)

a) If you've

been timed
and placed

for a parti

b) cular home-

coming-track
but no one'

s still wait
ing for you

c) there Most

likely you've

failed to
notice those

last-minute–

d) changes or you'

ve gotten–out
on the wrong

side of the
station With

e) only an old-

fashioned

radio and a
simple tele

phone not to

f) mention his pre-

electric type
writer he's

easily dated
to the late 50

g) s or early 60

s as he's been

left with that
world behind

with only his

h) poet's pen to

resist that
time–initiat

ing future
Or perhap

i) s indicate

another re–

activating
route for poet
ry's renew

ing course.

With closed (2)

    a) windows keep

    ing these e

    ver–insisting
    winds empty-

    breathed The
    spring's daily

    b) rising sun'

    s enabled to

    warmth to the
    very depth of

    our futur
    ing-hope

    s.

Chinese (4)

a) poetry seem

s even at

its high
tides to have

b) assembled

its own for

modern not
Chinese read

ers imaged–

c) symbols or

an exclusive
if for us

but obscure
ly hermetic

d) learned-re

semblance

to our own
poetic now–

says.

Looking (3)

    a) down that dark

    ening pond

    near the Scars
    dale Public Lib

    b) rary He knew

    unseen fish

    would still
    be swimm

    ing there in

    c) the very-depth

    of his own
    silent self–

    withdraw
    ing instin

    cts.

There are mo (2)

> *a) ments in life*
>
> that seem to
>
> inhabit them
> selves as a
>
> public heroic
> monument to
>
>
> *b) a long-since-*
>
> forgotten
>
> but once time
> ly-appropri
>
> ate-leader.

This early (2)

> *a) spring sky'*
>
> s continual
>
> ly retained
> its pre-estab
>
> lishing poet
> ic-dialogue

b) Constable

duly aware of

that calling
it by a name

less alway
s varying wind-

scheme.

Only the *(6)*

a) wind remains

unanswered

though it a
lone seems most

b) actively pre

sent Does it

alter its lang
uage according

to seasonal

c) change and daily

initiative
s If so its

most subtlety
grammared

d) It also never

seems purpose

ly receptive
except perhap

s at its in

e) visible origin

s Is that why

it alone seem
s incapable

of a meaning

f) ful dialogue

Yes only the
wind remain

s continual
ly unanswer

ed.

This morning' (3)

a) s most diffi

cultly arrange

able clouds
have moment

b) arily disappea

red while an

indefinite
blue has taken

their place
Perhaps we

c) should call on

a Constable

to rearrange
them again in

his own most
personal way?

The bared- *(3)*

a) sensed branch

es of this

high-rise
non-flower

b) ing tree left

his early morn

ing thought
s extending

even beyond
reach of

c) where they'

d left this

star-clear
wintered-

night distant
ly-awaken

ed.

Mrs Hofmann (5)

a) at 93 a redis

covered new

friend all a
lone with her

b) off-track se

cluded house

and her near
by fully self–

perpetuat

c) ing family at

mercy's–length
daily reclaim

ing the best
of music she'

d) d soloisted

in her early

Dresden-years
and a living

e) faith trans

cending even

her weaken
ing body–

claim
s.

Hide and seek *(6)*

a) Beware upon

entering this
Rosemarie'

s birthplace–

b) house there

may be just
around the

corner a
poem resid

c) ing its

own dialogued

cause that o
vercame his

steadfast

d) self-assum

ing certain
ing resist

ance That's
perhaps part

e) ially why

he succeed

s in such
hide and seek

relation
s with most

f) any and every

small child

subwayed if
only short-dis

tancing
s.

On Track *(3)*

a) Daily in need

of keeping

his own self-
sustaining

b) thoughts on

track because

they alone
realize the

familiari

c) ties and dis

tancings of
such newly

time-sponsor
ing endeavor

s.

If poets re (2)

a) main at best

gold-seeker

s the waste
of those daily

deepening-ex
cursions

b) must be spent

bare until

the gold a
lone shines

through its
secluded-in

habiting
s.

They Warren *(7)*

a) and Carol

(most essent

ial to the
only group I

b) ever felt a

part of)

simply sold
their house

packed-up
and left no

c) one knows why

(if I wasn't a

part of the
blame) with

only that part
ing evening

d) meal at The

Boat House

left to dine
upon past-re

membrance

e) s One should

n't feel poss
essive about

friends — (we
all ship-out

f) sometime or

other) but

their loss
and Leroy'

g) s knifed at

his library

left a not-
so–healsome

vacancy.

Looking-out (3)

a) this color-

rich(ly) in

viting win
dow I began

b) to feel my

self almost

as one of
those budd

ing tree

c) s also in

the white
of dressed–

out poetic
time–spell

s.

Gastronomics *(8)*

a) Ingo remain

ed (as far as
I know) our

only friend
with a most

b) ly pre-arrang

ed agenda We

needn't wait
for such theme

s to evolve
with their own

c) activating

time–length

s we found
them tasteful

ly waiting
for us as

d) Solvey's or

Rosemarie'

s 5 course
fully–attend

ing achieve–

e) ment-banquet

s The accompan
ing first-class

cuisine helped
at times to

f) sweeten rather

than spice-up

the contrast
ing aesthetic

taste of S. L.

g) and ourselve

s as we quest

ioned the
post-Christian-

untouchably
tolerant humane

h) wishful-think

ingness of

the so-called
Enlighten

ment.

Challenged *(4)*

a) Nothing quite

so unbeholden

even unbalanc
ing for my

b) liberal fa

ther and myself

as being forth
right challeng

ed by an appar

c) ently venomous

womanly-counter
part He winced

I remember

d) only that once

from his authori
tative high-stool

ed monied-pre
sence.

"In the groove" (3)

a) perhaps what

Tony means when

I've written
my dialoguing-

b) self into

where there's

a non-stop
nor looking-

back but strai
ght-on the

c) not quite fully-

paved word-de

lineating
accessible

bi-way
s.

The ease of

a momentary
pause reflect

ing whatever
seems focus

ed to one's
shortly-sens

ed express
ive word-need

s.

Big theme (3)

    a) s are most

    often poetic

    ally sourced
    through less

    b) significant

    examples as

    love sensed
    only by the

    intimate

    c) touch of hand

    s or even a
    knowing eye-

    length respon
    se.

If because (3)

    a) of Corona

    there's really

    nowhere left
    to go one can

    b) significant

    ly distance

    even little
    known terrain

    by just sit

    c) ting still

    reflecting
    this or that

    past or pre
    sent.

Satisfact

> ion can best
> be realized
>
> by just lett
> ing time
>
> settle-down
> to your own
>
> life-inhal
> ing quietude
>
> s.

Wallace Stevens' (2)

> *a) "Two Letters"*
>
> achieve an in
>
> timacy of word-
> expressive
>
> ness that leave
>
> *b) s nothing or*
>
> even little
> left that re
>
> mains to be
> necessar
>
> ily-said.

Dramatic (4)

    a) pathos of the

    Beethovian

    kind while per
    haps quite

    b) effective

    in its own

    right and way
    But I'd still

    prefer at least

    c) in my aging

    years the spir
    itual linear–

    fluency of
    the Rennaiss

d) ance master

s as Palestri

na and the
somewhat dark

er-hued Victor
ia.

Good and

effective kiss
es flow into

those sensual
streams of a

life-awaken
ing aware

ness.

It still look (3)

    a) s cold to me

    through these

    glass-faced
    windows when

    b) the mid-after

    noon late March

    sun retires
    and those sharp-

    insistent-wind
    s are left

    c) free-reign

    over our pre-

    determining
    sensibilit

    ies.

Two-wayed (3)

    a) Willing to

    die most espec
    ially because

    death's willing

    b) for him yet

    holding-on
    for dear-life

    a two-wayed
    person as all

    c) believer

    s with the

    living and re
    surrected

    Christ.

If one does (5)

a) n't know what

should be

said it's bett
er to say

b) nothing at

all Let him

path you to his
own way bet

ween life and
death holding

c) a balance

that's never

theless strong
ly pre-deter

mined If it'
s the last

d) time you'll

hear his voice

remember it
with a rever

ence for his
person and con

e) stant faith

as a candle

he held high
until it had

become complete
ly burnt–

down.

Yes he'll be (4)

a) remembered

for a Christ

ian school
he founded

in times of

b) a waning faith

For his publish
er's awareness

of a danger
ously expanding

militant Islam

c) For his lectur

er's actively
propagating

biblical
faith Our last

ing friend
ship's still

d) alive even if

he's drifting

alone in a time
lessly prepar

ed harbour
of his own.

Imagine (6)

a) the unspoken

tension of

Sperling’
s fallen–in–

love with his

b) best friend’

s wife an un
revealed in

timacy that
shadowed

his coming

c) s and going

s especial
ly when hous

ed in a comm
on together

d) ness. Klemper

er the famed

linguist marr
ied to a German–

European cult
ure while deny

e) ing his Jewish

ness even when

faced by a
Nazi blood–

proof hidden
through those

f) dire year

s until re

birthed again
German not Jew

ish.

Suspicion (3)

a) even when un

founded as

jealousy as
in Shakespeare'

b) s Othello poi

sons one's

very nerve-
length until

as often acti
vated into a

c) misrespresen

ted self-in

criminating
dangerous

behavior.

Take side (4)

> *a) s red or green*
>
> blue or grey
>
> red or blue
> But what if

> *b) you're divid*
>
> ed right-down-
>
> the-middle as
> in so-called
>
> "border state

> *c) s" when even*
>
> family loyality'
> s questioned
>
> or as that
> paella-waiter

d) in Garda grand

parented by 4

different
nationali

ties.

He knew he (2)

a) was being watch

ed our across-

the-way
neighbor had

begun to test-
him-out the

b) who what why

of my contin

uous early-
morning acti

vating type
writer even

spy-like.

Polonius' (4)

    a) advice an

    extra room

    or two good
    books an act

    b) ively walkable

    dog and a renew

    ing marital re
    lation the

    best mean

    c) s of getting

    out of this
    closed–in

    shut–out

d) claustropho

bic feeling
caused by Cor

ona's world–
wide hegemony.

A dog's life *(3)*

a) Not only the

Spanish dog'

s life refus
al for con

b) tinuous anti

Corona–walk–

outs but e
ven Matthew'

s California'

c) s emphatic

dog friend'
s not a step

or paw-length
further.

Unrequited *(8)*

a) wishful-think

ing If only

this through-
telling cold

b) ly-emphatic

wind would

just quiet-
down for a

while of cap

c) tivating

and even time-
prevading

stillness
es If ever I

d) became a dicta

tor of taste

as Reich-Ran
icki or Joach

im Kaiser I'
d immediate

e) ly disown my

wayward influen

ce exchanged
for Emerson'

s indespensible
essay on self-

f) reliance.

No doubt

that a deeply
self-reveal

ing Christian
raison d'être

g) can alter one'

s tasteful possi

bilities The
real question'

s whether
that already

h) prevailing

taste wasn't

indicating
the way for a

timely Christ
ian-awakening.

Those Fox Mead (4)

a) ow's Elementary

School's high–

flying swing
s taught him

quite young

b) that one should

n't try to ex
ceed one's

ground–based
self–securing

time–hold

c) though as a

child high–
flyer he soon

discovered
that on the

swings had

d) become trans

lated into
poetic light-

calling per
suasion

s.

At time *(2)*

a) s it seem

s easier to

misunder
stand what'

s said than

b) to realize

a commonly-
shared word–

appreciate
ing express

ion.

Drowsing (3)

a) off into

an extended

mid-day sleep
somehow remind

s me of what

b) the ancient

s described
as Hades

but then
there's no

boatsman

c) here to warr

ant me through
to the hard

ly time-secur
ing other

side.

Rosemarie' (2)

a) s gladness-re

ceptive-smile

somehow sub
conscious

ly motivate

b) s more of

my prolific
poeticness

than either
she nor I

could realize
how and why.

Are my hand (3)

    a) s marked with

    prior indeli

    ble experien
    ces of their

    kind or o

    b) ther Or are

    they to be
    read in a

    future estab
    lishing time-

    frame-of-re

    c) ference Or

    were they
    themselves

    always so
    self-reveal

    ing.

Are cat

s simply play
ful or are

they especial
ly cat and

mouse sadist
ic or does

that display
two side

s to their
same instinct

ive-behavior.

History (5)

a) Does history

end with that

most subject
ive "what

b) actually

happened"

or does it
become more-

so and other
wise through

c) changeable

times and

self-accomo
dating histor

ians It could
have been o

d) therwise but

it wasn't

yet what
could-have-

been remains
just as evid

e) ent through

dreams and

those painful
time-reflect

ive moment
s.

Corona (3)

> *a) 's not only*
>
> evident world–
> wide but in
> Europe's off–
> shore Britain
>
>
> *b) it's chosen*
>
> both the prime
> minister and
>
> the heir–to–
> the–throne
>
> to prove that
>
>
> *c) it's become*
>
> personally
> dangerous
>
> to deny its
> invisible po
>
> tency.

Are most all (4)

a) men personal

ly suscept

able to a Don
Giovanni life-

style but re

b) main domestical

ly home-bred
for lack of a

(shall we call
it) manly cour

age Jacob later

c) called "Israel"

remained a per
sonal home-stay

er because
he realized

The Good Lord

d) favored and

furthered
such a fam

ily–orient
ed behavior.

2*nd* *Command (4)*

a) ment (Moses)

The "enlight

ened" liberal
theologian

b) s have recreat

ed the biblical

holy and thor
oughly untame

able God in the

c) image of their

own wishful-
thinking as

the harmless

d) always forgiv

ing sweetly at
tuned baby-Jesus

Christmas-pack
aged.

This spring' (4)

a) s weather-wise

as a woman un

able to certain
her ever-change

b) able mind-

set fewer

insects fewer
birds – per

haps they're
still vacation

c) ing in the South

but with such

a variety of
innocently

colored–flow
ers adorning

d) this early spring-

time's ground–

base and tree
climbing–pleas

urings.

They (the often (2)

    a) quoted so-call

    ed experts) say

    the next war
    will be sound

    lessly invisib
    ly fought Per

    b) haps Corona'

    s a fore–taste

    of that enemy'
    s tactic's

    snake–like
    changeabil

    ities.

Trump seem (3)

    a) s quite adept

    at enemying

    our once trad
    itional demo

b) cratic Europ

ean allies

because his
"America first"

's attuned to
the only kind

c) of repertoire

congenial for

him economic
and not polit

ically.

At least a (5)

a) nother month

of being im

prisoned
in this no–

b) ways-out

Domestic vio

lence's on the
rise most

everywhere

c) even if dis

tances from

our time–
attending

roadside–

d) hearing One'

s reminded of
solitary–con

finement but
now for "two'

e) s for tea

and tea's for

two" alias with
out the most–

necessary
sugaring.

The natural (4)

a) reaction to

such a complete

loss of basic
freedom as to

b) rebel but in

side's the only

refuged place
left from this

hauntingly

c) effective in

visible virus
We're not able

now to kill it
or even fully

d) protect ourselv

es or even to

touch its de
vastating post-

democratic
power–control.

Perhaps one (4)

a) cause of my

(as it now

seems) endem
ic prolific

b) ness is the

variety of my

most personal
ly known inti

mate reader
s They're more

c) there than I

realize how

most especial
ly Rosemarie

while their
mind-sense at

d) times careful

ly watching

if only in
the still re

levant-back
ground.

Historical (4)

> *a) events Calling*
>
> them histori
>
> ical events
> usually because
>
>
> *b) of their unique*
>
> purposing
>
> s should never
> deny what's of
>
> daily import
>
>
> *c) yet newly per*
>
> spectived His
> tory's more like
>
> those mountain
> streams dried
>
> summer-down

d) but then awak

ened to
their fresh

ly-watered
listening–ap

peals.

Quick in *(2)*

a) sights as the

sudden flash

of sunlight
on water may

well describe
the birth of

b) a poem but it

still needs–be–

bodied with a
dialogical

self–suffi
ciency.

Yes as Shakes (2)

> *a) peare in his*
>
> incomparable
>
> sonnets and as
> the finest Tang
>
> poets need in

> *b) their own way*
>
> conclusive
> couplet-end
>
> ings I'm lin
> ed-up right–
>
> behind-them.

If my poetry' (4)

> *a) s better than*
>
> I am Why when
>
> the choice is
> given do I

b) prefer a close

personal relat

ion with those
unable to appre

ciate my poetry

c) to one with a

depthed poeti
cal understand

ing but lack
ing in a per

d) sonal soul-

sense Must I

requestion
my own pre–

given priori
ties.

Another grey (3)

    a) in grey fully

    self–conceal

    ing day as Li
    Schangyin's "her

    b) metic poem

    s" What or

    who is he hid
    ing from and

    who'll convinc

    c) ingly decode

    those so often
    apparently un

    related symbol
    ic image

    s.

March 29 *(7)*

    a) Doris' birth

    day six-and-a

    half years old
    er than her

    b) spoiled-brat-

    of-a-brother

    The great fam
    ily emancipa

    tor as she

    c) often proclaim

    ed from our
    parent's more-

    than-efficient
    timely lock-

d) hold She remain

ed before and

after schooling
and her highly

vocal marriage
a double sided

e) person always

with a book

of compelling
social subtle

ties in hand

f) most especial

ly Henry James
and Jane Austen

but she a top-
notch student

g) at Smith and Rad
cliffe so often

so quickly e
motionally

sparked–off.

Praying so (3)

a) often for his
sick and dy

ing friend
s also a sub

terranean way

b) of implying a
thankful
ness for all

that held–him–
here healthy ground–

based with his

c) lovely and lov

ing wife and an
inexplainably

prolific poet
ic daily-awaken

ings.

As those (2)

a) Breughelian

hunters on the

scent for a
book-finaliz

ing poem that
would satisfy

b) him and his

dialoguing

hound-dogs
as a troph

aed home-
sake.

P. S. (2)

a) Was Saint Cor

ona a double-

agent Sainted
not only be

cause of her
help in time

b) s of pando

mined Corona'

s now turned
against her

own name-
sake.

*In Nomine
Domini!*

March 29, 2020

Poetry books by David Jaffin

1. **Conformed to Stone,** Abelard-Schuman, New York 1968, London 1970.

2. **Emptied Spaces,** with an illustration by Jacques Lipschitz, Abelard-Schuman, London 1972.

3. **In the Glass of Winter,** Abelard-Schuman, London 1975, with an illustration by Mordechai Ardon.

4. **As One,** The Elizabeth Press, New Rochelle, N. Y. 1975.

5. **The Half of a Circle,** The Elizabeth Press, New Rochelle, N. Y. 1977.

6. **Space of,** The Elizabeth Press, New Rochelle, N. Y. 1978.

7. **Preceptions,** The Elizabeth Press, New Rochelle, N. Y. 1979.

8. **For the Finger's Want of Sound,** Shearsman Plymouth, England 1982.

9. **The Density for Color,** Shearsman Plymouth, England 1982.

10. **Selected Poems** with an illustration by Mordechai Ardon, English/Hebrew, Massada Publishers, Givatyim, Israel 1982.

11. **The Telling of Time,** Shearsman Books, Kentisbeare, England 2000 and Johannis, Lahr, Germany.

12. **That Sense for Meaning,** Shearsman Books, Kentisbeare, England 2001 and Johannis, Lahr, Germany.

13. **Into the timeless Deep,** Shearsman Books, Kentisbeare, England 2003 and Johannis, Lahr, Germany.

14. **A Birth in Seeing,** Shearsman Books, Exeter, England 2003 and Johannis, Lahr, Germany.

15. **Through Lost Silences,** Shearsman Books, Exeter, England 2003 and Johannis, Lahr, Germany.

16. **A voiced Awakening,** Shearsman Books, Exter, England 2004 and Johannis, Lahr, Germany.

17. **These Time–Shifting Thoughts**, Shearsman Books, Exeter, England 2005 and Johannis, Lahr, Germany.

18. **Intimacies of Sound,** Shearsman Books, Exeter, England 2005 and Johannis, Lahr, Germany.

19. **Dream Flow** with an illustration by Charles Seliger, Shearsman Books, Exeter, England 2006 and Johannis, Lahr, Germany.

20. **Sunstreams** with an illustration by Charles Seliger, Shearsman Books, Exeter, England 2007 and Johannis, Lahr, Germany.

21. **Thought Colors,** with an illustration by Charles Seliger, Shearsman Books, Exeter, England 2008 and Johannis, Lahr, Germany.

22. **Eye-Sensing,** Ahadada, Tokyo, Japan and Toronto, Canada 2008.

23. **Wind-phrasings,** with an illustration by Charles Seliger, Shearsman Books, Exeter, England 2009 and Johannis, Lahr, Germany.

24. **Time shadows,** with an illustration by Charles Seliger, Shearsman Books, Exeter, England 2009 and Johannis, Lahr, Germany.

25. **A World mapped-out,** with an illustration by Charles Seliger, Shearsman Books, Exeter, England 2010.

26. **Light Paths,** with an illustration by Charles Seliger, Shearsman Books, Exeter, England 2011 and Edition Wortschatz, Schwarzenfeld, Germany.

27. **Always Now,** with an illustration by Charles Seliger, Shearsman Books, Bristol, England 2012 and Edition Wortschatz, Schwarzenfeld, Germany.

28. **Labyrinthed,** with an illustration by Charles Seliger, Shearsman Books, Bristol, England 2012 and Edition Wortschatz, Schwarzenfeld, Germany.

29. **The Other Side of Self,** with an illustration
by Charles Seliger, Shearsman Books, Bristol,
England 2012 and Edition Wortschatz,
Schwarzenfeld, Germany.

30. **Light Sources,** with an illustration by Charles
Seliger, Shearsman Books, Bristol, England
2013 and Edition Wortschatz, Schwarzenfeld,
Germany.

31. **Landing Rights,** with an illustration by Charles
Seliger, Shearsman Books, Bristol, England
2014 and Edition Wortschatz, Schwarzenfeld,
Germany.

32. **Listening to Silence,** with an illustration by
Charles Seliger, Shearsman Books, Bristol,
England 2014 and Edition Wortschatz,
Schwarzenfeld, Germany.

33. **Taking Leave,** with an illustration by Mei Fêng,
Shearsman Books, Bristol, England 2014 and
Edition Wortschatz, Schwarzenfeld, Germany.

34. **Jewel Sensed,** with an illustration by Paul Klee,
Shearsman Books, Bristol, England 2015 and
Edition Wortschatz, Schwarzenfeld, Germany.

35. **Shadowing Images**, with an illustration by
Pieter de Hooch, Shearsman Books, Bristol,
England 2015 and Edition Wortschatz,
Schwarzenfeld.

36. **Untouched Silences**, with an illustration by Paul
Seehaus, Shearsman Books, Bristol, England 2016
and Edition Wortschatz, Schwarzenfeld.

37. **Soundlesss Impressions**, with an illustration
by Qi Baishi, Shearsman Books, Bristol, England
2016 and Edition Wortschatz, Schwarzenfeld.

38. **Moon Flowers**, with a photograph by Hannelore
Bäumler, Shearsman Books, Bristol, England 2017
and Edition Wortschatz, Schwarzenfeld.

39. **The Healing of a Broken World**, with a
photograph by Hannelore Bäumler, Shearsman
Books, Bristol, England 2018 and Edition
Wortschatz, Cuxhaven.

40. **Opus 40**, with a photograph by Hannelore
Bäumler, Shearsman Books, Bristol, England 2018
and Edition Wortschatz, Cuxhaven.

41. **Identity Cause**, with a photograph by Hannelore
Bäumler, Shearsman Books, Bristol, England 2018
and Edition Wortschatz, Cuxhaven.

42. **Kaleidoscope**, with a photograph by Hannelore
Bäumler, Shearsman Books, Bristol, England 2019
and Edition Wortschatz, Cuxhaven.

43. **Snow-touched Imaginings**, with a photograph
by Hannelore Bäumler, Shearsman Books, Bristol,
England 2019 and Edition Wortschatz, Cuxhaven.

44. **Two-timed**, with a photograph by Hannelore
Bäumler, Shearsman Books, Bristol, England
2020 and Edition Wortschatz, Cuxhaven.

Book on David Jaffin's poetry: Warren Fulton,
Poemed on a beach, Ahadada, Tokyo, Japan and
Toronto, Canada 2010.